MAKE HISTORY
ANCIENT EGYPT

**RECREATE AUTHENTIC JEWELRY, TOYS, AND OTHER CRAFTS
FROM ANOTHER PLACE AND TIME**

by Nancy Fister and Charlene Olexiewicz

Illustrations by Elizabeth Stubbs

Photographs by Ann Bogart

Lowell House
Juvenile

Contemporary Books
Chicago

Publisher: Jack Artenstein
Vice President, Juvenile Division: Elizabeth Amos
Director of Publishing Services: Rena Copperman
Managing Editor, Juvenile Division: Lindsey Hay
Editor in Chief, Juvenile Division, Nonfiction: Amy Downing
Art Director: Lisa Theresa Lenthall
Models: Stephanie Neumen, page13; Michael Olexiewicz, page 32

Library of Congress Catalog Card Number is available.

ISBN: 1-56565-516-8

Lowell House books can be purchased at special discounts when ordered in bulk for premiums and special sales. Contact Department JH at the following address:

Lowell House Juvenile
2020 Avenue of the Stars, Suite 300
Los Angeles, CA 90067

Manufactured in the United States of America
10 9 8 7 6 5 4 3 2 1

CONTENTS

A WORD ON HEIROGLYPHICS

Unlike the English language, each hieroglyphic symbol could represent one or more letters, a whole word, or even an idea, such as a god or the afterlife. This made it possible to "spell" a word with letters or with a symbol. There were no vowels. There were several different types of hieroglyphics used. While examples are included in a few crafts, you may want to find some other books on ancient Egypt and experiment with various other hieroglyphic alphabets.

INTRODUCTION

The land of Egypt was a hot, dry desert. However, within this seemingly desolate area, the ancient Egyptian culture thrived and left behind a vast amount of art, architecture, and written records. Today, we are able to piece together information about the Egyptian people, one of the most accomplished and longest lasting civilizations of the world.

Egypt was ruled by a long line of kings, also called pharaohs, who were believed to be gods in human form who ruled on earth. The royal throne and title of king passed from father to son, or to a daughter's husband. (A royal headdress can be created on page 30.)

Towns along Egypt's Nile River banks used the river's floodwaters to irrigate the land for farming. The Egyptians also became very skilled boat builders and fishermen, traveling up and down the river. (Make your own papyrus boat on page 20.)

The Egyptian religion honored many gods and goddesses. The people believed that the gods had power over everything, including the underworld—the place to where the dead traveled before moving on to their next life. The Egyptians prepared the dead for this "afterlife" by mummification—embalming and wrapping bodies to preserve them. (Build a mummy on page 8.)

As you create the projects in this book, you will see that there are many things about the ancient Egyptians that make them similar to us. They built monuments and statues, paid taxes, played music, and spent time with their families.

Grab your paints, glue, and other craft materials, and learn more about ancient Egypt as you MAKE HISTORY!

CORN HUSK BALL

Egyptian children played with many toys that you would recognize—tops, dolls, board games with dice, and balls of various sorts. Since there was no plastic or rubber in ancient Egypt, balls were often formed by rolling vegetable fibers, such as the husks of corn and grain, very tightly. They were secured by wrapping flax string around them. Flax string is made from the flax plant that grew in the marshes along the Nile River. Last, the ball would be covered with leather sections, similar to our tennis and baseballs. Balls were also made of wood and baked clay. They may not have been perfectly round, but they were brightly colored and striped. Most of the Egyptian balls were fairly small and could fit in a child's hand.

MATERIALS

- dried corn husks
- paper towels
- twine
- measuring tape
- tracing paper
- scissors
- pencil
- straight pins
- 9" x 12" piece of felt
- embroidery floss and needle

DIRECTIONS

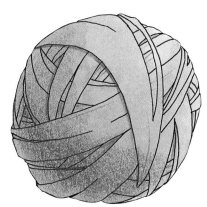

1 Dry the corn husks by laying them on a few paper towels. They take a day or two to dry. Roll the dry corn husks tightly, winding each one around the core in a different direction to form a round ball approximately the size of a tennis ball.

2 Wrap the corn husk ball with twine. Continue wrapping in different directions until the ball measures $9^3/4$" in circumference. (To measure the circumference of a ball, wrap measuring tape around the middle of the ball. The measurement where the tape meets itself is the circumference.)

3 On a piece of tracing paper, trace the pattern shown on page 6. Cut your pattern out on the solid line. Pin the pattern onto the felt with straight pins and cut out. Do this five times.

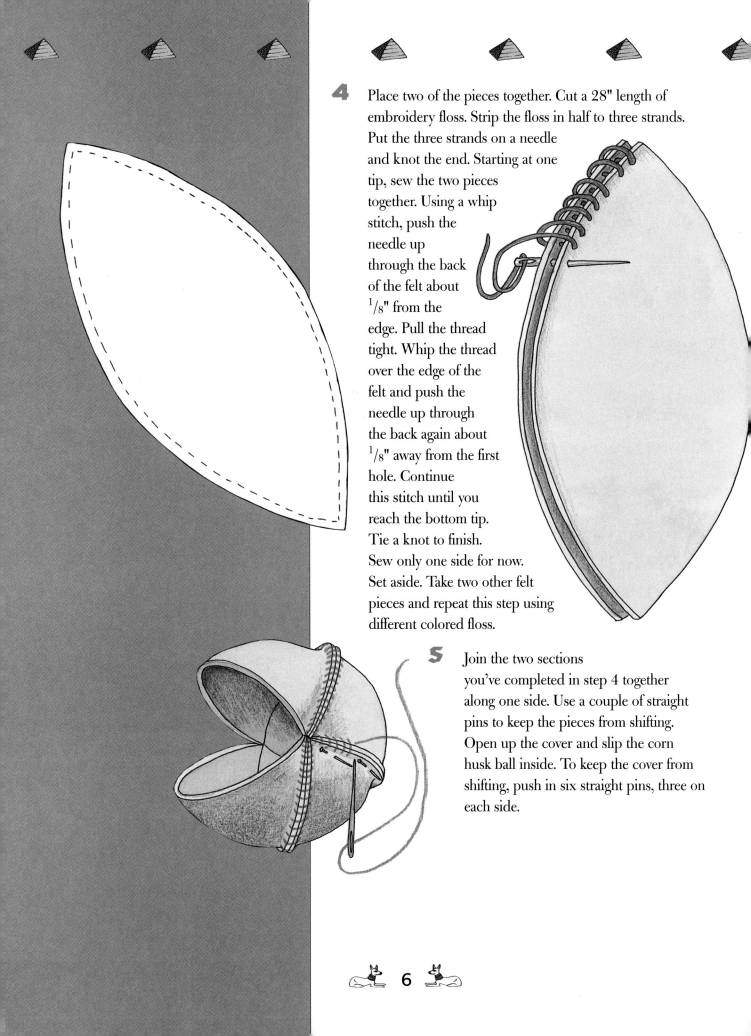

4 Place two of the pieces together. Cut a 28" length of embroidery floss. Strip the floss in half to three strands. Put the three strands on a needle and knot the end. Starting at one tip, sew the two pieces together. Using a whip stitch, push the needle up through the back of the felt about $1/8$" from the edge. Pull the thread tight. Whip the thread over the edge of the felt and push the needle up through the back again about $1/8$" away from the first hole. Continue this stitch until you reach the bottom tip. Tie a knot to finish. Sew only one side for now. Set aside. Take two other felt pieces and repeat this step using different colored floss.

5 Join the two sections you've completed in step 4 together along one side. Use a couple of straight pins to keep the pieces from shifting. Open up the cover and slip the corn husk ball inside. To keep the cover from shifting, push in six straight pins, three on each side.

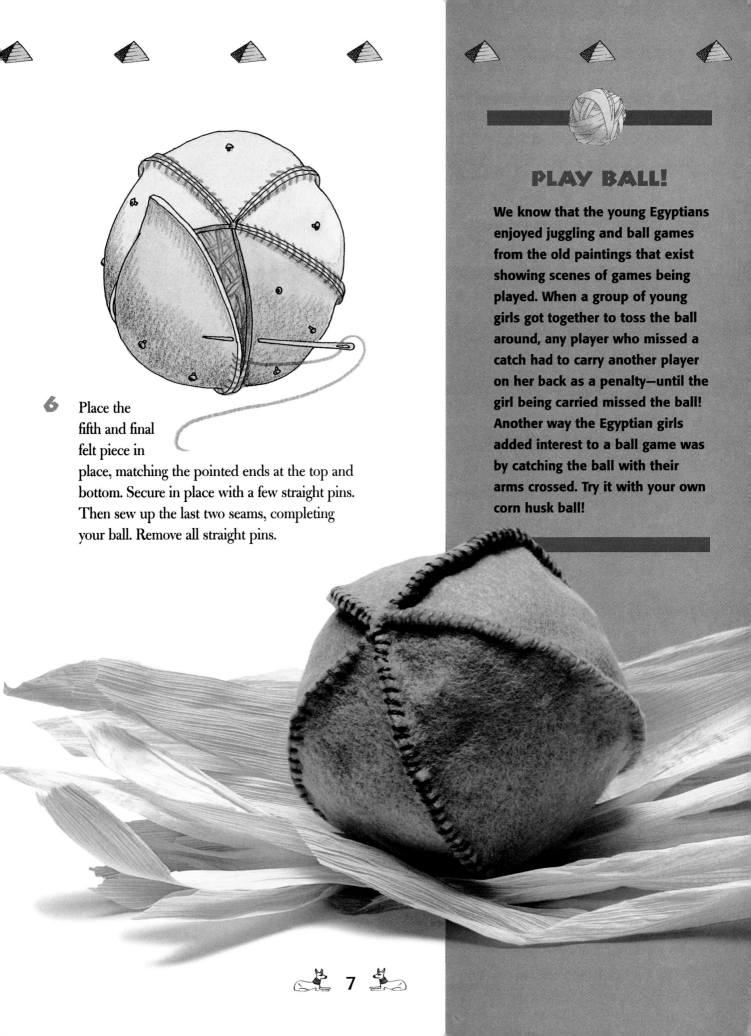

6 Place the fifth and final felt piece in place, matching the pointed ends at the top and bottom. Secure in place with a few straight pins. Then sew up the last two seams, completing your ball. Remove all straight pins.

PLAY BALL!

We know that the young Egyptians enjoyed juggling and ball games from the old paintings that exist showing scenes of games being played. When a group of young girls got together to toss the ball around, any player who missed a catch had to carry another player on her back as a penalty—until the girl being carried missed the ball! Another way the Egyptian girls added interest to a ball game was by catching the ball with their arms crossed. Try it with your own corn husk ball!

PAPIER-MÂCHÉ MUMMY

One of the most amazing traditions of the Egyptians was their process of mummification. They believed that by preventing the decay of the physical body, the soul of the person—which left the body at death—would be able to identify the body and return to it for the afterlife.

The process of mummification began with the removal of all the internal organs. Once the body was completely dried out, spices, straw, linen, and bitumen—a tarlike residue that hardened into a glassy black substance—were packed into the body cavity. This was followed by the artful wrapping of the body from head to toe with strips of linen, dipped in a sticky resinous substance. Layer upon layer was wound around the corpse as a priest chanted special prayers. The more important the person, the longer the layering process. The wrapping of a king could take months, while a common person would receive far less attention, perhaps not being preserved at all.

MATERIALS

- newspaper
- scissors
- tape
- ¼ cup flour
- ¼ cup water
- bowl
- masking tape
- white drawing paper
- water-based paints, including gold
- paintbrushes
- pencil

DIRECTIONS

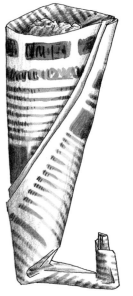

1 Wad a piece of newspaper into a ball for the head. Roll a sheet of newspaper into a pointed ice-cream cone shape. Fold the pointed end over toward the wide end once or twice to form the feet with toes pointed up.

2 From the wide end, trim the cone off to create an 8" body. Stuff a few newspaper scraps inside the cone. Tape the feet in place and the head to the shoulders (the wide end of the cone). Set aside. Mix flour with water in the bowl to make the papier-mâché paste. The paste should be a thick consistency.

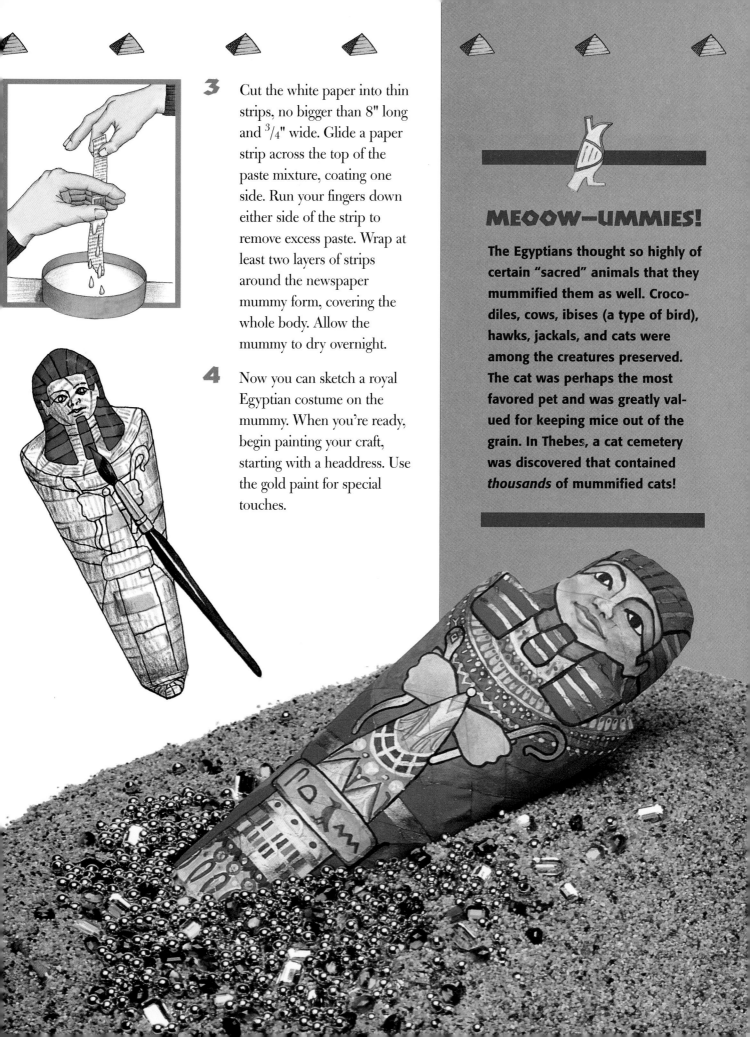

3 Cut the white paper into thin strips, no bigger than 8" long and ³/₄" wide. Glide a paper strip across the top of the paste mixture, coating one side. Run your fingers down either side of the strip to remove excess paste. Wrap at least two layers of strips around the newspaper mummy form, covering the whole body. Allow the mummy to dry overnight.

4 Now you can sketch a royal Egyptian costume on the mummy. When you're ready, begin painting your craft, starting with a headdress. Use the gold paint for special touches.

MEOOW—UMMIES!

The Egyptians thought so highly of certain "sacred" animals that they mummified them as well. Crocodiles, cows, ibises (a type of bird), hawks, jackals, and cats were among the creatures preserved. The cat was perhaps the most favored pet and was greatly valued for keeping mice out of the grain. In Thebes, a cat cemetery was discovered that contained *thousands* of mummified cats!

PAINT A WALL FRIEZE

Colorful wall paintings called friezes, decorated the walls and ceilings of the king's palace, and the inside walls of the royal tombs. Paintings in the tombs sometimes depicted the important events in the pharaoh's life.

The paintings that have survived over the centuries have given us much information about Egyptian life. We have learned about the plants that grew in Egypt, the types of animals that lived then, and through paintings of the zodiac signs, we know that the Egyptians even studied astronomy.

MATERIALS

- black marker
- drawing paper
- masking tape
- newspaper
- waxed paper
- petroleum jelly
- plaster of paris
- bowl
- ¹/₂ pint water
- spoon
- butter knife
- paintbrushes
- acrylic craft paints, including gold
- tiny screwdriver (or awl)

DIRECTIONS

1 With the marker, draw a rectangle 5" x 6" on paper. Tape the paper down on a work table covered with newspaper. Place a sheet of waxed paper over the paper and tape it down. Smear petroleum jelly over the waxed paper.

2 To mix up a batch of plaster of paris, fill a bowl with ¹/₂ pint of water. Slowly sprinkle plaster into the water, until all the water is absorbed (about 4 cups). Stir with a spoon for about 3 minutes, until it thickens.

3 Spoon the plaster onto the waxed paper, staying within the lines of the rectangle, which is a guide only. With a butter knife, smooth out the plaster until it is about ¹/₂" thick. Leave the edges irregular looking. Allow it to dry overnight.

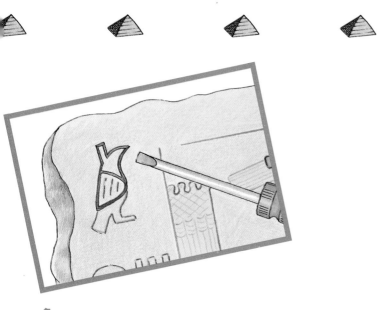

4 Pick the smoothest side to decorate and paint it a stone color. Allow it to dry. Sketch in a border design at the top and bottom (or sides) then paint it, and add a scene of your choice in the center. Pictures and hieroglyphs can also be incised or scratched on the frieze. To incise a design, have an adult help you use a tiny screwdriver to scratch into the surface.

DRAWING THE EGYPTIAN WAY

Here are some suggestions to imitating authentic Egyptian art.
- When you draw a person's body, or torso, face it front; but the arms, legs, and head should be drawn in profile.
- Since artists used size to show importance, the pharaoh was the biggest figure drawn. (Therefore, your most important object should be largest.)
- The Egyptians always used the same color for the same subject. Their colors were bold and solid, with no shading at all in their paintings.

BEADED COLLAR

Ancient Egyptian men and women of all ages and social classes wore jewelry. The common people used copper for necklaces, bracelets, earrings, headbands, and anklets, adding glazed beads, shells, polished pebbles, and grain seeds for decorations. All gold, which was found in great abundance in the sand along the Nile, belonged to the king. Royalty alone could wear the precious metal.

Necklaces and pins usually were worn for beauty and for the magical powers it was believed they gave to the wearer. Amulets, or charms, shaped like gods or goddesses supposedly shielded the wearer from harm. Amulets in the shape of animals were thought to transfer the characteristic of the animal, such as strength, to the person.

MATERIALS

- **Polymer (plastic) modeling clay (regular modeling clay may also be used)**
- **sharpened pencil**
- **acrylic craft paints**
- **paintbrush**
- **scissors**
- **colorful magazine pages**
- **glue**
- **cording (3 different colors: 2 at 4 yards long and 1 at 1¹/₂ yards)**
- **masking tape**

DIRECTIONS

1 Make twenty round beads, $^1/_2$" in size, from modeling clay. With the sharpened pencil tip, poke a hole in the center of each bead, about $^1/_4$" in size. Bake according to manufacturer's instructions. Paint the beads.

2 To make long beads, cut twenty triangles from colorful magazine pages as shown. Roll each triangle starting from the base toward the point. The hole in the center should be about $^1/_4$". Put a spot of glue at the point to secure it closed. Once dry, trim long beads to be $1^1/_4$" in length.

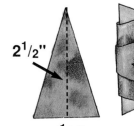

$2^1/_2$"

$1^1/_2$"

3 Take your three cords and wrap the ends with masking tape to keep them from unraveling. Knot the cords together 8" from one end. Lay them out flat with the short cord in the center. Knot the cords two more times as shown.

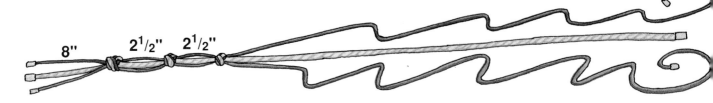

8" $2^1/_2$" $2^1/_2$"

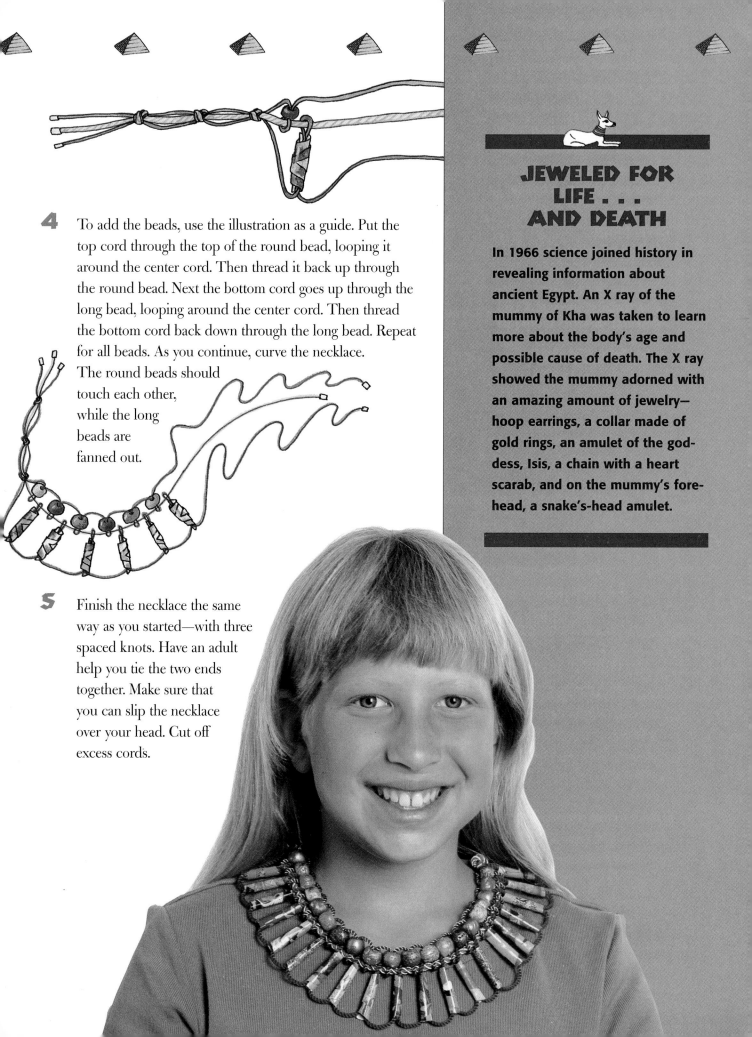

4 To add the beads, use the illustration as a guide. Put the top cord through the top of the round bead, looping it around the center cord. Then thread it back up through the round bead. Next the bottom cord goes up through the long bead, looping around the center cord. Then thread the bottom cord back down through the long bead. Repeat for all beads. As you continue, curve the necklace. The round beads should touch each other, while the long beads are fanned out.

5 Finish the necklace the same way as you started—with three spaced knots. Have an adult help you tie the two ends together. Make sure that you can slip the necklace over your head. Cut off excess cords.

JEWELED FOR LIFE . . . AND DEATH

In 1966 science joined history in revealing information about ancient Egypt. An X ray of the mummy of Kha was taken to learn more about the body's age and possible cause of death. The X ray showed the mummy adorned with an amazing amount of jewelry—hoop earrings, a collar made of gold rings, an amulet of the goddess, Isis, a chain with a heart scarab, and on the mummy's forehead, a snake's-head amulet.

SANDPAPER PYRAMID

The pyramids of ancient Egypt are among the world's oldest and most amazing structures. They were built as royal tombs for the pharaohs, whom the Egyptians believed were gods in human form. After death, the pharaohs supposedly returned to being gods. The triangular shape of the pyramid is said to signify the sun's rays as they stream to the earth, shining over the pharaoh. It was believed that the king could then climb up the rays to heaven.

For the Egyptians, life continued after death in the netherworld. To be prepared for the afterlife, the noble king was buried with food, clothing, jewels, furnishings, and many other fine things that he might want in the next life. The walls of the burial chamber were beautifully painted with hunting and boating scenes and stories from the king's life. To discourage thieves from stealing the wonderful treasures that were buried with the king, the pyramids contained passageways blocked with stone boulders, tunnels leading nowhere, and secret entrances. It didn't work; most of the pyramids have been robbed of priceless artifacts.

MATERIALS

- tracing paper, 16" square
- pencil
- right-angle ruler
- old scissors
- two 9" x 11" sheets of sandpaper, 100 grit
- glue
- white drawing paper
- colored pencils

DIRECTIONS

1 Draw two lines intersecting in the middle of the tracing paper as shown. Using the right-angle ruler, draw a $5^3/_4$" square in the center of the tracing paper.

2 Measure $4^1/_2$" out from the edge of the square on all four sides, placing dots on the horizontal and vertical lines. Draw straight lines from the dots to the corners of the squares. On opposite sides of the outermost square, draw in two tabs about $3^1/_2$" long and $1/_2$" wide.

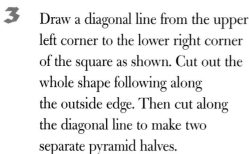

3 Draw a diagonal line from the upper left corner to the lower right corner of the square as shown. Cut out the whole shape following along the outside edge. Then cut along the diagonal line to make two separate pyramid halves.

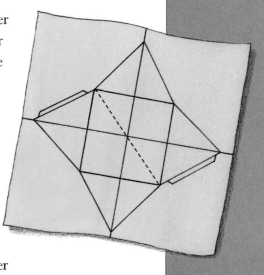

4 Using one of the pieces as a pattern, lay it on the smooth side of a sheet of sandpaper. Trace around the edges, then cut out the shape. Repeat with the other piece of sandpaper.

5 Fold the triangle points of the sandpaper up to form the sides of the pyramid. Fold the tab toward the smooth side of the sandpaper. Apply glue to the tab and fasten the two pyramid sides together. Repeat with the other half of the pyramid.

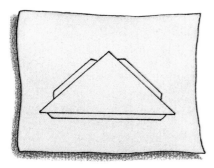

6 To make the interior wall, take the white drawing paper and draw a line 8" long for the base of a triangle. Find the center point of the line (4" in from either end) and using the right angle, make a dot $3^5/_8$" above the center point. Connect the dot to the ends of the base line, forming a triangle.

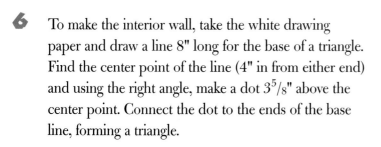

7 Draw tabs 4" long and $^1/_2$" wide on both sides of the triangle, then one long tab 7" long and $^1/_2$" wide along the bottom of the triangle.

THE GREAT GIZA

The largest pyramid ever built was the Great Pyramid at Giza, which stands 500 feet high—more than the length of 1½ football fields—and covers 13 acres of ground! It was constructed of 2 million limestone blocks, each weighing about 2½ tons. It took over 20 years to build!

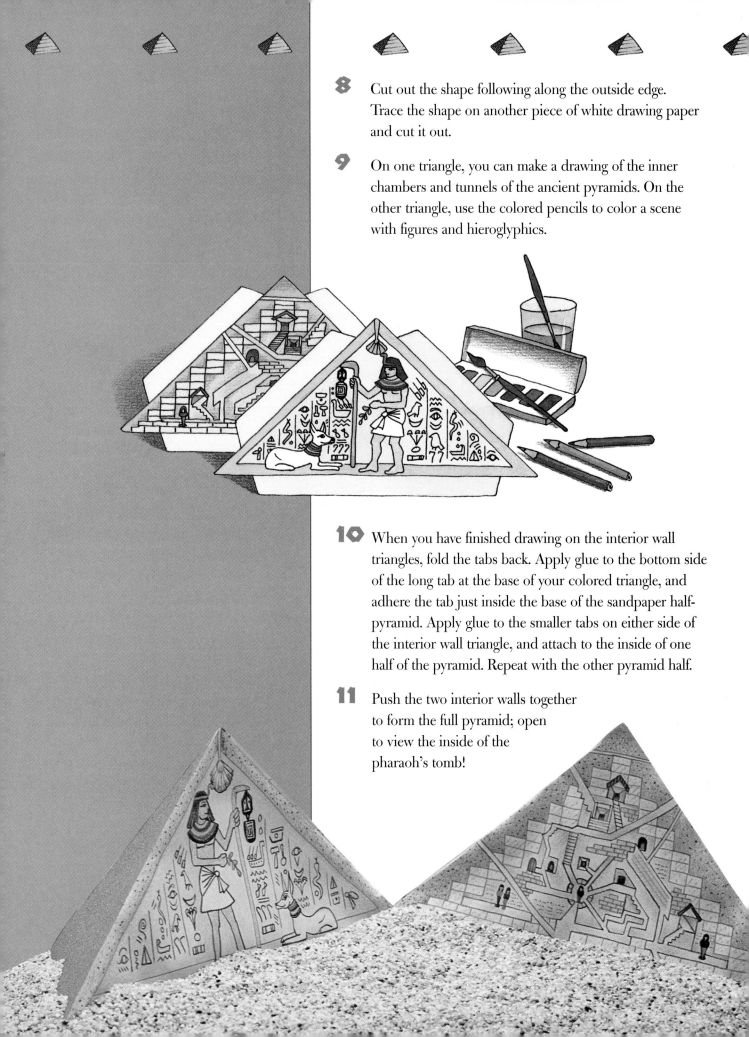

8 Cut out the shape following along the outside edge. Trace the shape on another piece of white drawing paper and cut it out.

9 On one triangle, you can make a drawing of the inner chambers and tunnels of the ancient pyramids. On the other triangle, use the colored pencils to color a scene with figures and hieroglyphics.

10 When you have finished drawing on the interior wall triangles, fold the tabs back. Apply glue to the bottom side of the long tab at the base of your colored triangle, and adhere the tab just inside the base of the sandpaper half-pyramid. Apply glue to the smaller tabs on either side of the interior wall triangle, and attach to the inside of one half of the pyramid. Repeat with the other pyramid half.

11 Push the two interior walls together to form the full pyramid; open to view the inside of the pharaoh's tomb!

TOOLS OF THE SCRIBE

The scribes of ancient Egypt were greatly respected, for they were advanced in their ability to read and write hieroglyphics, Egypt's unusual language of picture symbols.

The scribes kept records for the king, such as inventories of food supplies and the names and numbers of soldiers, craftsmen, and priests. Papyrus scrolls have also been discovered that contain medical information, law cases, magic spells, and even treatments for sick animals.

An experienced scribe wrote with brush and ink directly on papyrus—a paperlike material that the Egyptians developed from the papyrus plant—at least as early as 3000 B.C. The invention of paper greatly spread the knowledge of writing because the scrolls could be carried so much easier than the earlier heavy clay tablets.

MATERIALS

- 8¹/₂" x 11" white drawing paper
- old towel
- two tablespoons ground coffee and coffee filter
- rubber band
- coffee mug (half-filled with hot water)
- scissors
- white glue
- twigs, 9" or shorter
- clippers
- assorted color artist pastels (chalks)
- several sheets of sandpaper, 100 grit
- several small plastic containers (one for each pastel color)
- small cup of water
- aerosol hair spray

DIRECTIONS

1 Place two sheets of drawing paper flat on a towel. Heap two tablespoons of ground coffee onto the center of a coffee filter. Gather up the ends of the filter and tie with a rubber band. Place filter into a coffee mug half-filled with hot water. Allow it to sit until the water is cool.

2 Holding it by the rubber band, drag the filter back and forth across the paper as shown. Try to make streaks. Cover both pieces of paper and allow them to dry.

WHAT WAS IT LIKE TO BE A SCRIBE?

Boys as young as five years old could begin a career as a scribe. While they could look forward to a privileged occupation, unlike the hard, physical labor of the pyramid builders, it wasn't easy for the young boys to obey the strict demands of learning the profession. Every day they practiced copying the hieroglyphic symbols on pieces of broken clay, stone, or wooden tablets before they were allowed to work on the expensive papyrus paper. There were about 750 symbols in all. Compare this to the 26 letters in our alphabet!

3 Cut one streaked sheet into seven even horizontal strips. On the clean side of a paper strip, apply glue around the edges. Starting at the top, glue the paper strip to the blank side of the whole sheet. Continue gluing the strips row by row until done, then allow to dry.

4 To make the pens, find some stiff, thin twigs that would be suitable for writing tools. Have an adult help you cut the ends at a sharp angle using the clippers.

5 To create different colored inks, fold a piece of paper in half widthwise. Select one colored pastel stick and rub it over a piece of sandpaper, allowing the powder to fall onto the center of the paper. Rub until about $1/4$" of the stick is missing. Folding the paper in half again, carefully tip it into a small plastic container and pour out the powder. Repeat this step using a clean sheet of paper and a separate container for each color.

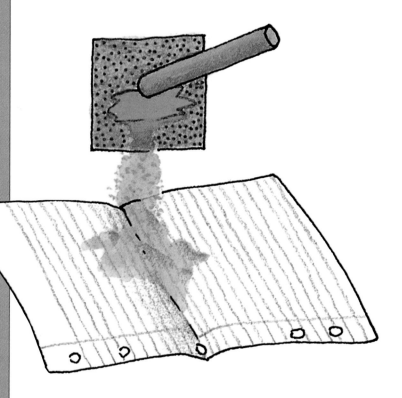

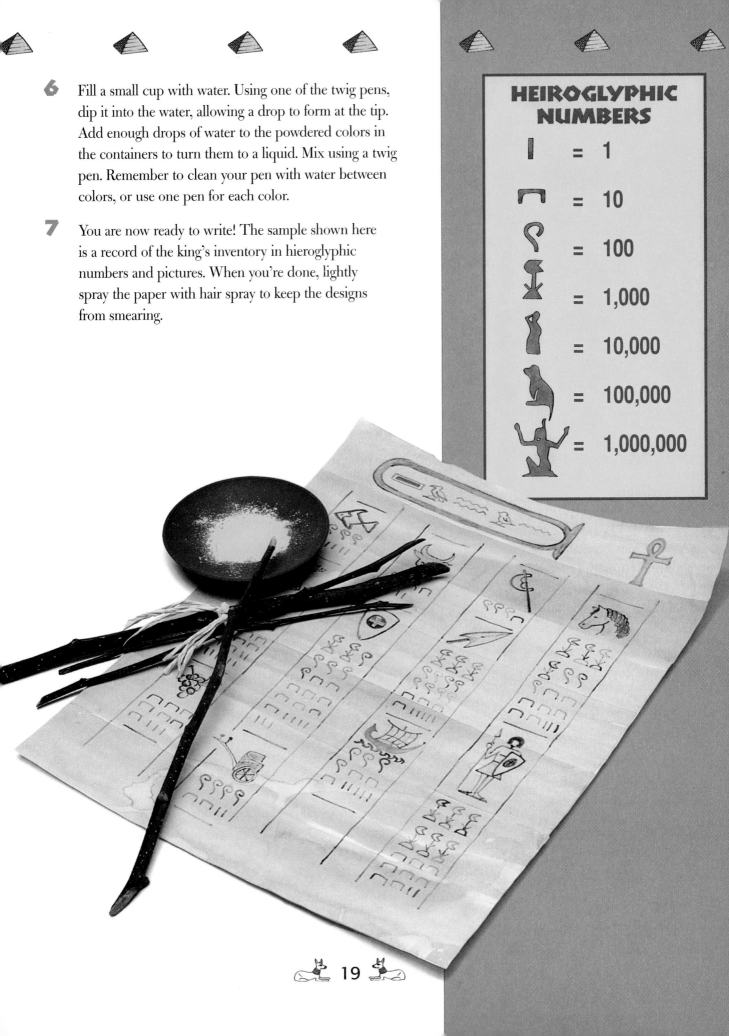

6   Fill a small cup with water. Using one of the twig pens, dip it into the water, allowing a drop to form at the tip. Add enough drops of water to the powdered colors in the containers to turn them to a liquid. Mix using a twig pen. Remember to clean your pen with water between colors, or use one pen for each color.

7   You are now ready to write! The sample shown here is a record of the king's inventory in hieroglyphic numbers and pictures. When you're done, lightly spray the paper with hair spray to keep the designs from smearing.

HEIROGLYPHIC NUMBERS

I	= 1
	= 10
	= 100
	= 1,000
	= 10,000
	= 100,000
	= 1,000,000

BUILD A BOAT

Living close to the Nile River made boats very important in Egyptian life. The earliest style of boat was a simple and small reed boat called an ambatch (AM-bok). To make an ambatch, the Egyptians tied together bundles of papyrus and grasses that grew along the sides of the river. Similar to a canoe with a reed mat for a floor, the ambatch held only one person.

Eventually the Egyptians traded gold and food for cedar wood from inland areas. From the wood, they constructed sturdy barges to carry cattle and heavy stones for building pyramids. These barges had to be pulled by several smaller boats.

MATERIALS

- scissors
- 6 yards of ivory-colored paper twist
- old hand towel
- two 18" wires
- four rubber bands
- 4 yards string
- carpenter's wood glue
- ten Popsicle® sticks
- wire cutters

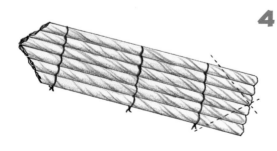

DIRECTIONS

1 Use scissors to cut six 12" lengths of paper twist, four at 20" each, and two at 24" each. Place the twists in a sink with water. Let them soak for 3 to 5 minutes, then place twists out straight on a towel. Tighten up the twists if necessary.

2 Cut three 10" lengths of string. Loop the center of one string around one of the twists, 2" from one end. Make sure the two ends of the string are even. Cross the string and pull to tighten.

3 Add another twist alongside the first one. Wrap string around the second twist, cross the string ends, and pull. Continue attaching twists until all six are connected. End with a knot. Repeat this step with the two remaining strings.

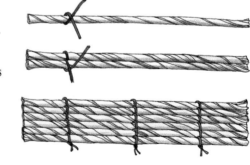

4 Cut the two boat ends into points as shown. This is the boat bottom. Set aside. Untwist one of the 24" lengths. Place one of the 18" wires on the paper and retwist the paper around the wire. Wrap both ends with a rubber band to secure. Repeat this step with the other twist and wire.

5 Cut six 8" lengths of string. Loop one string around the last twist of the boat bottom piece. Even up the string ends and cross. Add one of the 20" twists, centering it against the bottom piece. Attach another 20" length and then attach the twist with the wire. Add a string at the center and the other end. Repeat this step on the other side.

6 At one end of the boat, bend the two wired twists up and toward each other. Twist together. Now twist the four remaining pieces around the two wired ones. As you do this, the bottom pieces should be cradled inside. Wrap the end with a 12" length of string and knot. Repeat this step on the other boat end.

7 Glue two sets of four Popsicle sticks together. Now glue the sets together. When the boat is dry, glue the deck in the center.

8 Cut $1^1/_2$" off the end of a Popsicle stick, then split another Popsicle stick lengthwise. Trim it to $3^1/_4$" in length, and glue the two pieces as shown to make an oar.

SAILING WITH THE SUN

The Egyptians believed that the sun god, Ra, traveled across the sky in a boat with the sun. King Tut's tomb had a whole fleet of model boats meant to ensure that he would sail with Ra in the after-life. All the boats in his tomb pointed west, to the "magical place" where the sun god disappeared each night.

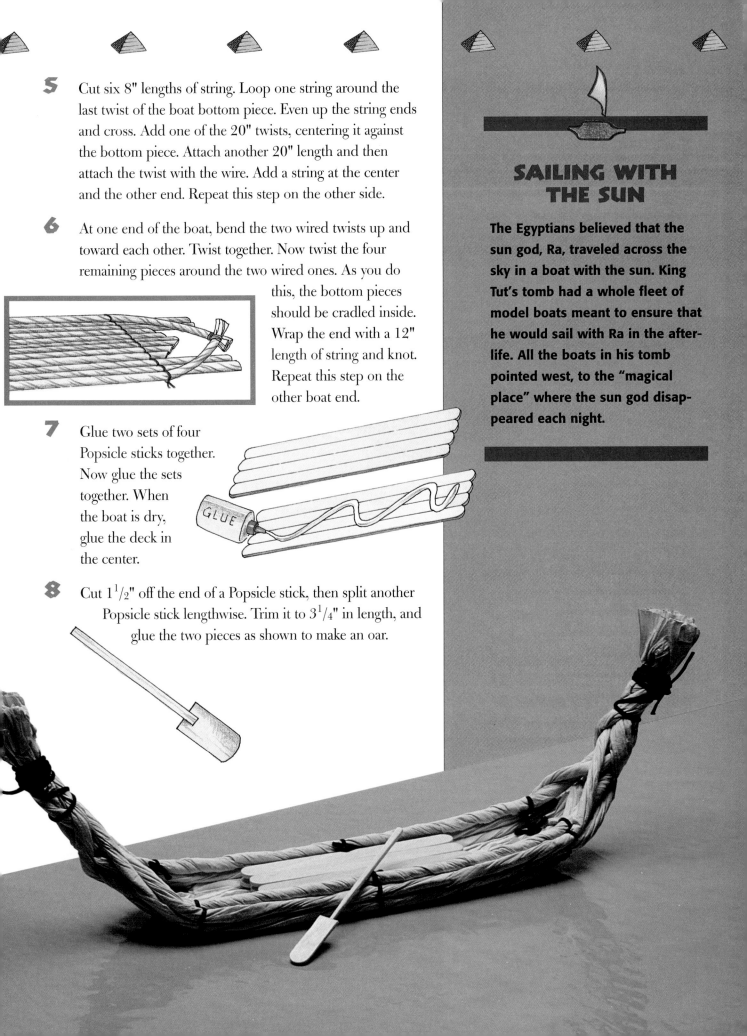

SCARAB SEAL

The Egyptian scarab was a stamp or seal molded in the shape of a beetle. The name scarab comes from the scientific name of the "scarabaeus" (scare-uh-BAY-uhs) beetle, a stout, brilliantly colored beetle common to ancient Egypt. Scarabs were made from a variety of materials, such as gold, bronze, semiprecious gems, wood, blue glass, and most common, clay.

On the bottom of the scarab, a person's name or a symbol that a person used to identify his property would be inscribed in the clay. The clay scarab could be attached to large jars of various household goods that were being stored in such a way that the scarab would have to be broken in order to open the jars. This would show an owner if someone had been robbing his supplies.

The markings on the bottom of the scarab could also be inked and stamped on important documents made from leather or papyrus, a paperlike material that the Egyptians developed from the papyrus plant.

MATERIALS

- tracing paper
- scissors
- modeling clay
- pencil
- paper clip or pointed stick
- paintbrush
- glue
- paint

DIRECTIONS

1 On tracing paper, create a symbol to be your personal mark. It should fit inside a $2^1/_2$" oval shape. Cut out the shape.

2 Make a ball with the modeling clay. Flatten it into an oval about $^1/_4$" thick and $2^1/_2$" long. With more clay, mold a second oval, flat on the bottom and curved on the top, into the shape of a beetle shell. Place the curved oval on top of the flat base. Gently press the two pieces together.

3 Take your drawn symbol and place it drawing-side down, on the flat bottom of the scarab. Trace over your design with a pencil. (It will appear backward on the scarab. When you print it, it will be correct!) Using the paper clip or stick, design a few lines on the rounded beetle shell. Then turn it over and engrave your personal mark on the flat bottom, going over your pencil marks. Let the clay dry overnight.

4 With a paintbrush, spread a *very* thin layer of glue on the flat bottom and allow it to dry. This will keep the paint from being absorbed into the porous clay. Brush a thin layer of paint on the scarab bottom and print your hieroglyphic initials on the paper. Rinse or wipe off the paint each time you change colors, but don't soak your clay scarab, as it may soften!

THE MAGICAL SCARAB

When mummies were wrapped, a stone scarab was sometimes put near the heart. Magical spells carved on the scarab were meant to aid the deceased in the underworld when his or her heart was weighed against the Feather of Truth on a scale to measure its good deeds in life. To ensure a happy afterlife, the heart must balance perfectly with the feather. The inscription on the scarab begged the heart not to betray its owner.

MAKE A SISTRUM

Music, dancing, and love were the characteristics of the Egyptian goddess Hathor. In the ancient tomb paintings, Hathor often held a sistrum in her hand, a type of rattle with metal disks strung on a slender wire. When shaken, the disks made a tinkling percussive sound, like today's tambourine. The specific use of the instrument is not known for sure. It appears that only women played it, perhaps because one of the uses was in the worship of Hathor, considered a devoted mother and wife, who assisted with safe childbirth.

MATERIALS

- scissors
- poster board
- pencil
- awl or nail
- magazine
- carpenter's wood glue
- $3/4$" thick wooden dowel, 8" long
- thumbtack
- light brown acrylic craft paint
- paintbrush
- two aluminum foil pie plates
- stiff 16-gage wire
- wire cutters
- pliers

DIRECTIONS

1 Cut poster board into each of the following dimensions: A) $1^1/_2$" x 18"; B) $1^1/_2$" x 5"; C) $1^1/_2$" x 6". Mark each strip with its proper letter, **A**, **B**, or **C**. On strip A, mark three dots at 2", $3^1/_2$", and 5" from each end and centered. Use the awl to punch holes at these marks just big enough for the wire to slip through. Place a magazine under the strips to protect the tabletop.

2 On strip B, make a line 1" from each end, across the strip. Fold the two ends up along the lines. Bend A into an arc. Glue the inside ends of A to the outside ends of B. Cut a hole in the center of strip C the same size as the dowel. Make a line 2" from each end, across strip C. Fold ends up along the lines. Glue C to outside of A, leaving a 1" gap between B and C.

3 Apply glue to the top of the wood dowel. Push the dowel through the hole in C until it rests against strip B. To further secure it, stick a flat thumbtack in the top of B to go through the dowel. Paint the sistrum frame and allow to dry.

2"
$3^1/_2$"
5"

A

B

4 Cut twelve $1\frac{1}{2}''$ squares from the foil plates. The cut edges are sharp, so have an adult help you. Use the nail to punch holes in the center of each square, again placing a magazine underneath the aluminum.

5 Cut three 6" lengths of wire. Push one wire through the bottom hole on one side of the sistrum. String four foil squares onto the wire. Now push the wire through the bottom hole on the other side. Use pliers to bend one wire end down and the other end in a loose S shape. Repeat for the remaining wires.

C

ENCHANTING EGYPTIAN MUSIC

Along with sistrums, the Egyptians also played lutes, harps, lyres, flutes, and tambourines to accompany songs for religious celebration and for social banquets. Existing paintings show wives playing for their husbands, and women playing instruments, dancing, and clapping their hands at the royal court. However, some historians think at some point, women may have taken over the profession from men. Making music was one of several occupations open to women outside the home, though probably a job of low status.

ROYAL CARTOUCHE

Whenever you see the oval cartouche (kahr-TOOSH) in an Egyptian scene, you know a very important name is written inside it—the name of an Egyptian king or god. The very shape of the cartouche was the hieroglyphic symbol for *name*. Cartouches were inscribed on tomb walls, painted on mummies, carved on stone coffins, or worn around the neck as a magic amulet to ward off evil or injury to the wearer. By placing a person's name on his mummified body or coffin, it was believed to make him live again in the next world. The hieroglyphic writing inside the cartouche could be written either horizontally or vertically.

MATERIALS

- scissors
- white or gold poster board
- colored pencils
- white glue
- colored craft sand
- gold cord or piping
- Popsicle® stick

DIRECTIONS

1 Cut a piece of poster board measuring 3" x 6". Round off the four corners. About $1/2$" from the bottom, have an adult cut out a $1/2$" wide slit, about 1" long. Draw hieroglyphics to spell out your name or initials. Color in the symbols.

2 Mark off a $1/4$" border around the edge of the cartouche. Carefully, but quickly, spread a thin layer of white glue throughout the background of the cartouche. Be careful not to spread glue into the $1/4$" border or onto the hieroglyphs.

3 Sprinkle colored craft sand over the entire cartouche. When dry, tip the cartouche over and lightly tap to remove excess sand. Glue gold cord around the outer edge of the cartouche.

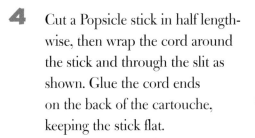

4 Cut a Popsicle stick in half lengthwise, then wrap the cord around the stick and through the slit as shown. Glue the cord ends on the back of the cartouche, keeping the stick flat.

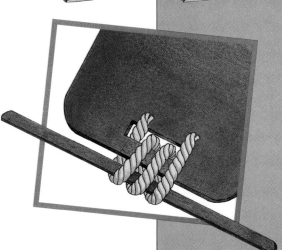

CRACKING THE CODE WITH A CARTOUCHE

For many years after the Egyptian civilization had disappeared, no one could understand the meaning of the hieroglyphics. Then, in 1799, a broken slab of stone called the Rosetta stone was discovered in Rosetta, a town near Alexandria, Egypt. A message was written on it in three different scripts. Nobody could figure out what the message meant. The name of an ancient ruler, Ptolemy, written inside a cartouche, was recognized in one of the languages, finally allowing the unknown code of the hieroglyphic symbols to be broken.

PADDLE DOLL

The paddle doll must have been a favorite toy of Egyptian girls, as many dolls have been found buried in their tombs. Both adults and children had only their most special possessions in life buried with them.

Made from a flat piece of wood, the paddle doll body was decorated with painted patterns and designs, and pictures of animal gods. Hathor, whose many characteristics included dance, love, and joy, was often portrayed on dolls' bodies with the head or horns of a cow. The paddle doll had a full head of hair made from many strands of mud beads.

MATERIALS

- pencil
- 8" x 15" foam core board, ¼" thick
- Exacto® knife
- glue
- one large Popsicle® stick
- acrylic craft paints
- paintbrush
- thirty ³/₈" (10mm) wooden beads
- scissors
- black yarn
- 8" length of wire
- masking tape
- wire cutters
- assorted color embroidery floss (optional)

DIRECTIONS

1 Draw the doll shape shown here on the foam core board. Have an adult cut out the shape and a 2" circle, using an Exacto knife.

2 Glue the circle onto the main head. Glue the Popsicle stick to the back side of the neck. Paint the wooden beads and set them aside to dry. Paint the entire doll with light brown acrylic paint. Once it's dry, sketch a geometric pattern on your doll, then paint it.

3 Cut 25 strands of black yarn, each measuring 26". Attach a strand onto the wire as shown. Pull tight. A small piece of tape over the first strand will help keep it in place. Attach remaining strands.

4 Push one end of the wire through the lower half of the top head piece (see **A**). Stop when 1" of the wire shows on the opposite side.

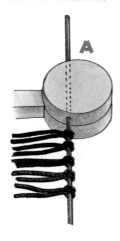

5 Bending the wire, bring the wire up over the top of the head until it crosses the other end (see **B**). Twist the ends together and trim excess with wire cutters.

6 Place the beads onto the yarn strands. Tie a knot at the end so the beads do not fall off. You can try braiding a few strands or adding accents of wrapped embroidery floss. Give hair a final trim to even it up.

WHAT OTHER TOYS DID EGYPTIAN CHILDREN HAVE?

Besides the paddle dolls for girls and toy soldiers for the boys, Egyptian kids had tops, glazed clay dolls, pull toys such as horses on wheels, animals with movable jaws—crocodiles and cows were popular—and small figures engaged in different activities such as rolling a ball, kneading bread dough, or washing clothes.

KING TUT'S HEADDRESS

Tutankhamen was just a boy of nine when he inherited the throne from his father-in-law, Akhenaton. He is believed to be the youngest king, and ruled for a relatively short period of time before his death at about age seventeen. King Tut, as he was called, was buried in the Valley of the Kings where many other rulers had their pyramid tombs built. But somehow Tut's tomb, though showing signs of minor break-ins, was resealed by Egyptian officials. It was never further looted by robbers, unlike most of the other royal tombs in the area. Some historians think his tomb may have been covered over by stone chips from the digging for the tomb of Ramses VI, another Egyptian king, located near Tut's.

In 1922 British Egyptologist Howard Carter discovered the steps leading down into the entrance gallery of Tut's tomb—and what a find! Tut's mummy was encased in three separate coffins. The outer two were covered in thin sheets of gold foil. The innermost one was made of solid gold an inch thick, and weighed over 2,500 pounds! When they opened his coffin, they found Tut's mummy wearing a pure gold funeral mask and a shoulder-length headdress. The headdress contained the royal symbols of the snake and the vulture. Tut also wore the false beard associated with the gods.

MATERIALS

- 1½"-wide gold ribbon, 16" long
- 1 yard striped fabric, 45" wide
- fabric glue (or glue gun)
- sewing needle and thread
- ¾"-wide elastic, 8" long
- scissors
- two 9" x 12" yellow foam sheets or poster board
- black puff and gold glitter paints (in writer-tip bottles)
- 9" length of wire
- wire cutters
- straight pins
- baby elastic cord, 24" long

DIRECTIONS

1 Center the gold ribbon on the long edge of the striped fabric. Be sure that the stripes run in the direction shown. Secure ribbon with fabric glue and allow to dry.

2 Have an adult or a friend help you with this step. With a needle and thread, attach one end of the ¾" elastic to the wrong side of the fabric near the end of the ribbon. Try the headdress on as shown on the next page, making sure the gold band is centered on your forehead right at your eyebrows. The gold band should cover the tips of your ears as you wrap the loose end of the elastic across the back of your head.

3 Pull the elastic until it meets the end of the gold ribbon on the other side, making the headdress snug. Hold your fingers on the elastic at this point, remove the headdress, and sew on the other end. Trim any excess elastic. Try on the headdress again, and have someone evenly trim the bottom edges of the fabric. Remove headdress.

4 Using the illustration as a guide, cut out two serpent shapes from a yellow foam sheet. With black puff paint, put eyes on one. On the other piece, use gold glitter puff paint to add the serpent's scales. Allow paint to dry.

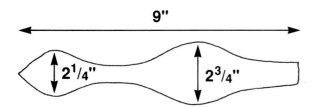

9"

2$\frac{1}{4}$"

2$\frac{3}{4}$"

5 Place the 9" wire down the center of one of the serpent's blank sides. Spread a generous amount of glue all over the surface, except for 1$\frac{1}{2}$" at the base. Place the other serpent piece on top (blank sides together). Allow glue to dry.

6 Bend the serpent into an S. Bend the 1$\frac{1}{2}$" unglued base to a vertical position. Ask someone to help you use wire cutters to trim off excess wire. Sew the serpent to the headdress in a few places to ensure that the serpent remains upright as shown.

WHAT DID HIS MUMMY UNCOVER ABOUT YOUNG KING TUT?

When Tut's mummy was examined, he was found to be wearing gold sandals, and each of his fingers and toes was topped with a gold cap. His body was adorned with jewels. From his mummy we know he was about 5'8" tall. He had long eyelashes and pierced ears. Though he died young, there were no visible signs of disease.

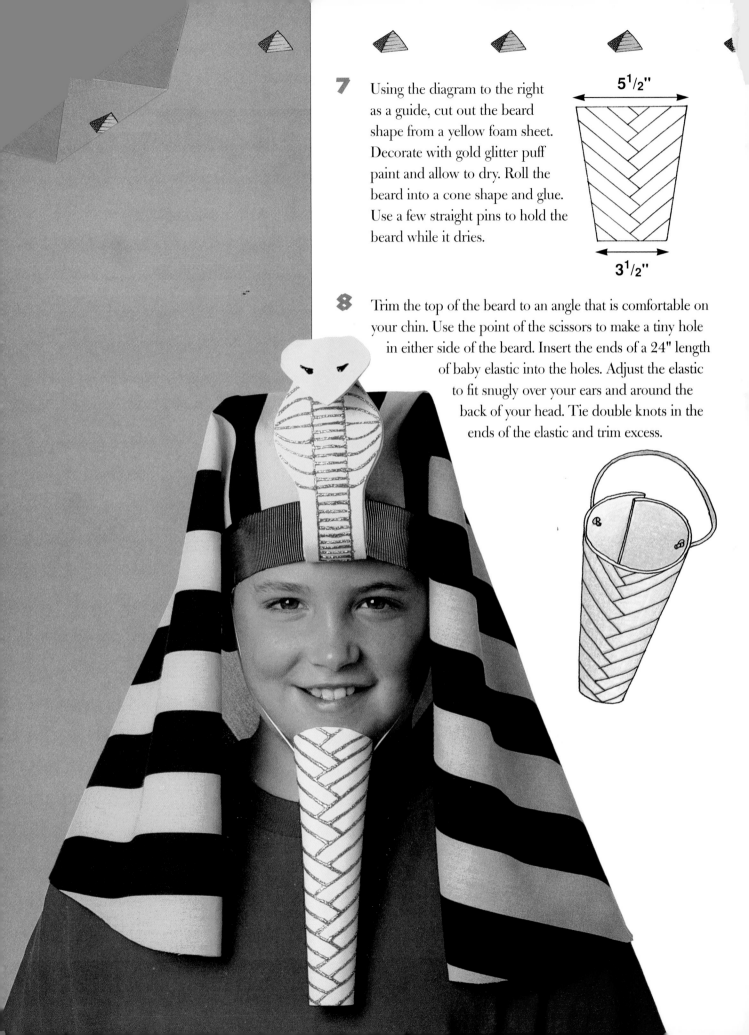

7 Using the diagram to the right as a guide, cut out the beard shape from a yellow foam sheet. Decorate with gold glitter puff paint and allow to dry. Roll the beard into a cone shape and glue. Use a few straight pins to hold the beard while it dries.

5¹/₂"

3¹/₂"

8 Trim the top of the beard to an angle that is comfortable on your chin. Use the point of the scissors to make a tiny hole in either side of the beard. Insert the ends of a 24" length of baby elastic into the holes. Adjust the elastic to fit snugly over your ears and around the back of your head. Tie double knots in the ends of the elastic and trim excess.